THE ABC's OF *Love* & *Relationships*

By:
Joseph Johnson

Copyright © 2018 by YAMsCreation

All rights reserved. No portion of this book may be reproduced-mechanically, electronically, or by any means, including photocopying without written permission of the publisher.

Library of Congress Cataloging-in-Publication data is available.

ISBN: 978-0-578-42219-0

Cover Design, Interior Layout & Co-Written with:
Yusuf A. Muhammad

If you are unable to order this book from your local bookseller, you may order directly from the publisher website.
www.YAMsCreation.net

YAM's Creation
P.O. Box 3196
Atlanta, Ga. 30302

This book is available at special rates when purchased in bulk for premium sales, sale promotion, for fund-raising or educational use. Special editions and books' excerpts can be created to specification. For details, contact the Special Sales Director at the email address:
Info@YAMsCreation.net

Printed in the United States of America
First Printing 2019

Table of Contents:

Forward   Page 7

The Way to Understand The Reading   Page 8

Principles

A.	*Accept*	page 13	O.	*Open Mind*	page 69
B.	*Balance*	page 17	P.	P-1 *Past*	page 75
C.	*Communication*	page 21		P-2. *Patience*	page 81
D.	*Dedication*	page 25	Q.	*Quit Complaining*	page 85
E.	*Equally Yoked*	page 29	R.	*Rest*	page 89
F.	*Forever*	page 33	S.	*Strength*	page 93
G.	*Genuine*	page 37	T.	*Trust*	page 97
H.	*Heaven*	page 41	U.	*Uniqueness*	page 101
I.	*Identity*	page 45	V.	*Value*	page 105
J.	*Journey*	page 49	W.	*We*	page 109
K.	*Know Your Mate*	page 53	X.	*X-Ray*	page 113
L.	*Loyalty*	page 57	Y.	*Youth*	page 117
M.	*Motivation*	page 61	Z.	*Zealous*	page 121
N.	*New Day*	page 65			

Additional Principle

"Rise Up"   page 127

Closing Thoughts   page 131
Cite Reference   page 133

This book is first dedicated to my children, through them I have gained patience and understanding. It is also dedicated to anyone seeking to make themself happy in an unhappy world.

> *"The first law of nature is self-preservation. Cut off that which may harm you. But if it is worth preserving, and is meaningful, nourish it and have no regrets. Ultimately, this is true living and love of self... from within."*
> — T.F. Hodge, From Within I Rise: Spiritual Triumph Over Death and Conscious Encounters with "The Divine Presence"

Because life is too short to wait for someone else to act right, make yourself happy...

Forward

The ABC's of Love & Relationships has been designed so that through the use principles one can assess their personal relationships while simultaneously allowing you to reflect upon your life views. This reading can be summarized as:

***The A**ffinity you have **B**uilt with another represented through **C**ommunication.*

Oftentimes, when you first meet a person, you do not meet the true version of that person, nor do they meet the true you. It is quite common for an individual to introduce you to their *Representative*. Who is that you may ask? This is the person they want you to like, want you to find interesting, and become attracted to. Many times, the "Representative" is the complete opposite of the individual you are going to discover. For this reason, many relationships end quickly, simply because most people are not truly honest from the beginning. However, there are a few that do last through this introductory phase. The question then becomes how do you make it work? How can you make it last?

Through asking questions to gain insight, understanding and feedback, as well as studying myself and others in various forms of relationships. My research has allowed me to discover that many of us do not have a clear concept of what love is. This book is designed not just as book but a workbook, because we must understand that building love and relationships with others takes work.

To Understand The Book, Please Read This Section First

This book is designed using the Alphabets as Principles for understanding; that if applied, can help you better your current relationship with self and others. Quotes are written throughout in gold to emphasis points. Each letter is broken down into Seven Elements: 1) for a better understanding of the Principle and 2) to help guide your thoughts and actions in wanting to be better. The Elements are:

1. ## *<u>The Letter</u>*

2. ## *<u>The Principle and Its Definition</u>*

A principle represents a fundamental truth or a proposition that serves as the foundation for a system of belief or behavior, or for a chain of reasoning

"A highly developed value system is like a compass. It serves as a guide to point you in the right direction when you are lost."
Idowu Koyenikan - Wealth for All: Living a Life of Success at the Edge of Your Ability

"Values are like a pilot's flight plan . . . without them you're flying blind."
Frank Sonnenberg - Follow Your Conscience:
      Make a Difference in Your Life & in the Lives of Others

The Principles are designed as a blueprint for you to focus on how you can lay your foundation and create your environment. These things are done by focusing on how you speak of yourself. Followed up by your actions and commitment, which helps you become what you are striving to be. The question you need to ask yourself is, "What is it that I am striving to be?" Not the lip service you're telling others, but the things you actually say and do. Your words and actions should mirror each other.

3. *Two Quotes*

The two quotes are designed as pre-thoughts to the explanation that will be given in hopes to guide your mind to where the reading is going. Think back to when you were in school and a teacher was getting ready to teach the class a new subject. Often the teacher did something first to draw your complete attention so they could introduce the subject matter, then they began their explanation. So it is with these principles. After they are defined, two thoughts are given as an introduction to where the reading is going. In order to properly understand the principles, your mind has to be open and not filled with your own perspective.

4. *An Explanation Of Why The Principle Is Important In Any Relationship.*

The essence of "Why" is the beginning and end of all things. William Barclay once stated, "*There are two great days in a person's life - the day we are born and the day we discover why.*" The same applies to relationships, the two great days are the day you enter into a relationship and the day you discover this is the right person for you. Once you have discovered your own reason, in most tasks, you begin to feel as if you're headed in the right direction. Yet if ones does not have understanding of why anything is being done, stated, or believed to be true, then they are doomed to failure. This book is designed to avoid future relationship failures. Though you may have your own opinion on the principles given, which may or may not be correct, still have an open mind when reading. This is suggested since you are evaluating how your opinion on the principle has been working for you thus far. Once you understand the why of your actions, you can properly move forward to get a better outcome for self. The goal of this book is for you to better understand yourself and obtain a better relationship with your mate and others. Friedrich Nietzsche said, "*He who has a strong enough why, can bear almost any how.*" Let's find your why in the relationship.

5. *Reflective Questions, To Ensure Understanding of Your Own Relationship*

Often we question others to gain insight and to better understand the logic in their reasoning. So why do we not take the time to learn about ourselves? If you understood why you had certain bad habits, would you make a conscious effort to change them? If you discovered the reason why you were missing the goals on tasks in your life, would you work to correct what's negative? Hopefully, the answer is yes. This philosophy of self-correction is used throughout this book. You have to look past the faults of others and begin to apply the ointment to the pain where it sometimes begins, WITHIN SELF.

I was once told, "*To get the right answer, you have to first ask the right question.*" By properly questioning self, you can get to the root of the problem and begin to change the negative in the situation. It will also help you to expand your thinking of the current relationship and of self. The questions are designed to develop your thoughts and actions, while offering reflective thinking that can help guide you to a better place.

6. *A Few Lines for You To Summarizes Your Thoughts*

Now it's time for you to go to work and write down your thoughts on the principles. Many points in your life this book may be used as a reference guide. However, each time you look at it, you will be able to see how far you have developed. Your present does not guarantee your future, and what you are today does not mean you will be that tomorrow. You have FREEDOM of choice, use it.

7. *W.O.W. (Words Of Wisdom)*

A personal reflection or insight from experiences on the subject, let these words inspire or encourage you.

Fundamental Thoughts on the Proper Development of ANY Relationship.

The motive of why you came together determines how long you will stay together...
– The Honorable Minister Louis Farrakhan

A person who looks everywhere but within for love misses the truest love there is, for the love you give your soul is one that cannot be replaced.
— Chizoma Cluff

Give Me An... **A**

Principle Accept

Defined: *To take or receive (something offered); receive with approval or favor*

*Letting go does not mean giving up,
but rather accepting that there are things that cannot be.*
– Unknown

You couldn't relive your life, skipping the awful parts, without losing what made it worthwhile. You had to accept it as a whole--like the world, or the person you loved.
– Stewart O'Nan

Why...

The most powerful six-word phrase you will ever hear is, *"Accept your own and be yourself."* Before you can properly enter a successful relationship with anyone, including yourself, you have to accept who you are as an individual. Whoever you are before you meet your potential mate is 70% - 90% the true you (we all have been influenced or changed by society). If you are a geek, be one and embrace it. If you are a lover of wild things, be yourself and believe that it is accepted by the right person. Do not change who you are, unless it is for the betterment of yourself. More specifically, do not change in order to get, please, or keep anyone else.

A

Reflective Questions

Who are you?
What flaws are you willing to accept from others?
What flaws are you willing to accept about yourself?

A Few Lines...

A

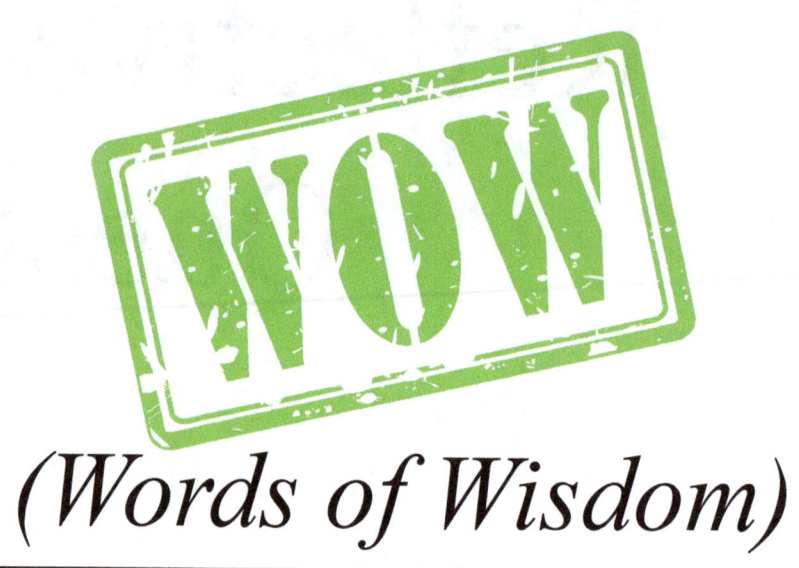

(Words of Wisdom)

For one to be properly accepted in any relationship, you NEED to KNOW YOUR LIMITS. Do not become a trashcan for others and an excuse maker for yourself. Always remember that the first law of nature is self-preservation.

Take care of yourself and know when enough is enough.

Give Me A.... **B**

Principle Balance

Defined: *An even distribution of weight enabling someone or something to remain upright and steady; keep or put in a steady position so that it does not fall.*

The heart and mind must work together or you will not find harmony in life, for without balance, you will be led astray.
— Unknown

It's all about quality of life and finding a happy balance between work and friends and family.
— Philip Green

Why...

To form a healthy relationship, a proper balance between work, family, friends, and other activities is necessary. When you enter a new relationship, particularly marriage, you are working to build a new bond. In order to properly get to know your mate, you need to spend quality time with each other outside of the bedroom. This will help strengthen the bond between the two of you. Therefore, in the beginning of the relationship, you should cut out as many individual and separate activities as possible so you can get to know each other better. You are supposed to be moving from the thinking of "I" to the thinking of "We". In order to successfully accomplish this transition, your thoughts and intentions must be followed up with sincere actions. Remember, *"If you want to go fast, go alone. But if you want to go far, go together."*

Reflective Questions

What is balance to you?
What are you willing to give up to develop a better relationship with self and others?
How much quality time do you spend with your mate versus by yourself or with friends?

A Few Lines...

(Words of Wisdom)

The balancing scale of weighing your relationship and your life is similar to any other scale that exists. On one side is the (actual) truth, and the other side is the truth we hope for (our version). To balance the scale, learn to see the truth in your actions versus what you believe at the moment. For many times your emotional beliefs, are the root of the problem. We "*feel a certain way*" about an issue instead of looking at the truth of it. Get out of your feelings and stand with the truth, it is always the safest ground to stand on.

Give Me A....

Principle C

Communication

Defined: *To share or exchange information, news, or ideas.*

The single biggest problem in communication is the illusion that it has taken place.
— George Bernard Shaw

You can change your world by changing your words... Remember, death and life are in the power of the tongue.
— Joel Osteen (Bible, Proverbs 18:21)

Why...

Communication comes in many forms, all of which are important because they can be the life or the death of the relationship. However, for any relationship to properly grow and develop, you NEED an open line of VERBAL communication between the two parties. One must be able to freely come to the other with questions, concerns, comments, and wondering thoughts. When your mate believes they can come to you to discuss whatever is bothering them without a fight, then you have helped to develop a key form of trust. Proper VERBAL communication can prevent others from meddling in your business, and create a stronger bond. Remember, when communicating for resolution, talk about the subject not around it.

Final Note: **TEXTING DOES NOT ALWAYS COUNT AS COMMUNICATION!**

Reflective Questions

*What is your mate's best way of telling you they love you? How do you respond?
What is your best way of telling them?
Do you listen to understand or to respond?*

A Few Lines...

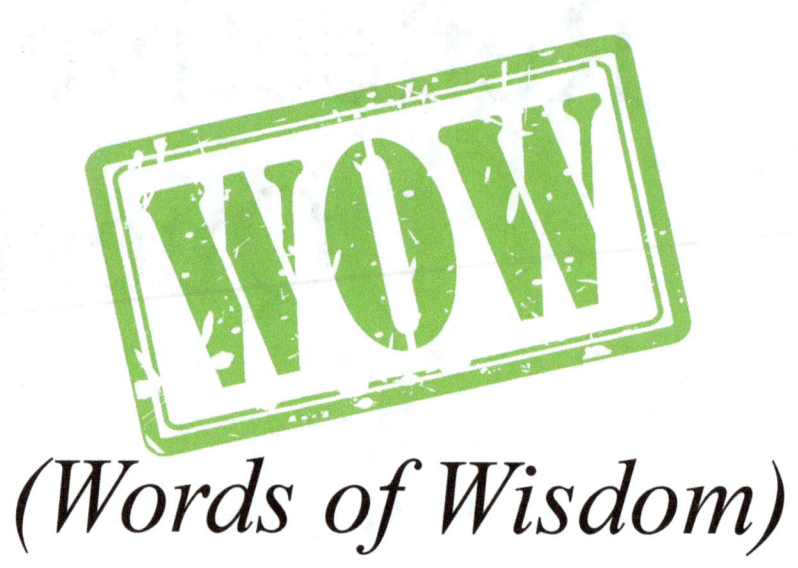

(Words of Wisdom)

WHAT you say to each other
is as equally important, as HOW you say it.

Many think this concept is trivial. However when you learn to speak to others how THEY WANT to be addressed, not the way YOU like to be addressed. The progression of your relationship can move swiftly. A good word can go further than any physical gift given. It serves as a better reminder during hard times in the relationship.

Give Me A.... **D**

Principle Dedication

Defined: *The quality of being committed to a task or purpose. Devote (time, effort, or oneself) to a particular task or purpose.*

Be all in or get out. There is no half way.
– Unknown

*If you really want to do something, you'll find a way;
if you don't you'll find an excuse.*
– Jim Rohn

Why...

The commitment you give to your significant other can determine the length and happiness of the relationship. To be dedicated to someone is explained best in the wedding vows, "For better or for worse, for richer or for poorer, in sickness and in health." In the simplest terms, it is to have an extended bond with someone at ALL times. Even when upset or frustrated with the other, your commitment is such that you will still continue to ensure their safety and happiness.

This principle represents a full-time job that doesn't allow part-time effort; especially if you want full-time results. If you don't have this kind of commitment, you should begin to figure out why your commitment is lacking? Either be all in or be out. Don't waste your time or others'.

D

Reflective Questions

How often have you allowed your emotions get in the way of checking on your mate's happiness?
What are the doubts you have in your mind about the relationship?
How do you plan to fix it?

A Few Lines...

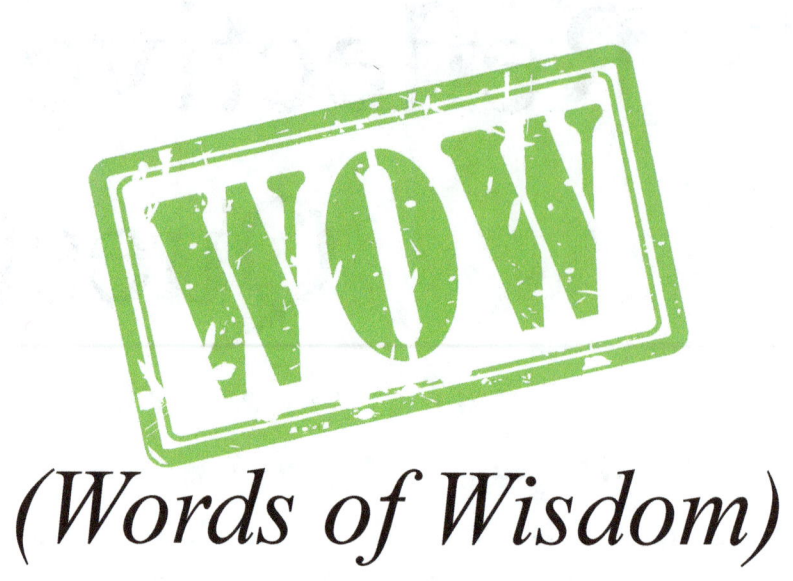

(Words of Wisdom)

Keep your mind on the goal! But first you need to know, ***"What is the Goal?"***

The goal is the reason you committed to the relationship, which shouldn't be sex or money. When times are rough, you have to remember the reason why OF ALL the people in the world, you chose your mate. Once you remember why you chose your mate, see if the reason still stands beyond the current situation. If the reason doesn't, decide whether you are staying or leaving and live with it. "Forever" can be changed by an incident of now, but make sure the reason is worth it.

Give Me An... **E**

Principle

Equally Yoked

Defined: *The idea that the individuals in a Christian relationship (or any other religion) are both committed to God.*

*Marriage equality is about more than just marriage.
It's about something greater.
It's about acceptance.*
– Charlize Theron

The yoke you wear determines the burden you bear.
– Edwin Louis Cole

Why...

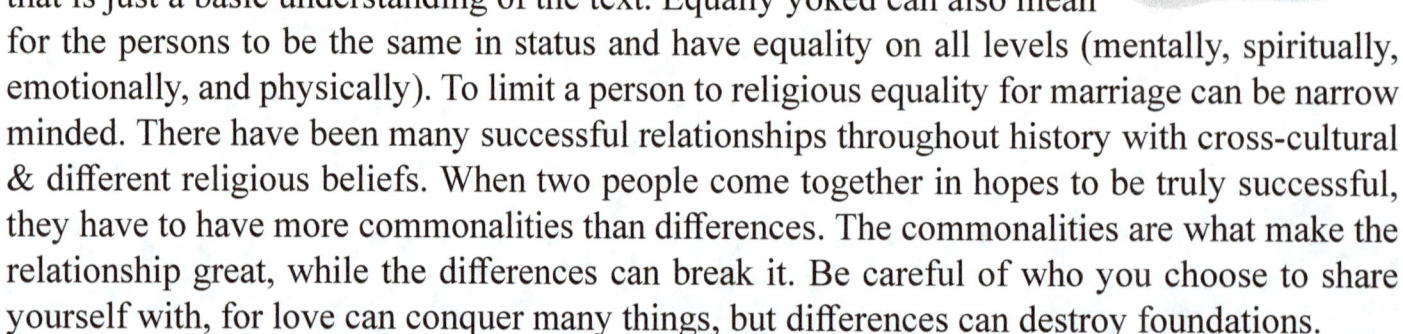

In 2 Corinthians 6:14, Paul speaks on being equally yoked, *"Be ye not unequally yoked together with unbelievers: for what fellowship hath righteousness with unrighteousness? And what communion hath light with darkness?"* Many think this scripture only refers to marriage; however, that is just a basic understanding of the text. Equally yoked can also mean for the persons to be the same in status and have equality on all levels (mentally, spiritually, emotionally, and physically). To limit a person to religious equality for marriage can be narrow minded. There have been many successful relationships throughout history with cross-cultural & different religious beliefs. When two people come together in hopes to be truly successful, they have to have more commonalities than differences. The commonalities are what make the relationship great, while the differences can break it. Be careful of who you choose to share yourself with, for love can conquer many things, but differences can destroy foundations.

Reflective Questions

How are you well rounded, equally yoked, as a couple?
What are your commonalities and differences?
Can you last happily with them? How do you know?

A Few Lines...

E

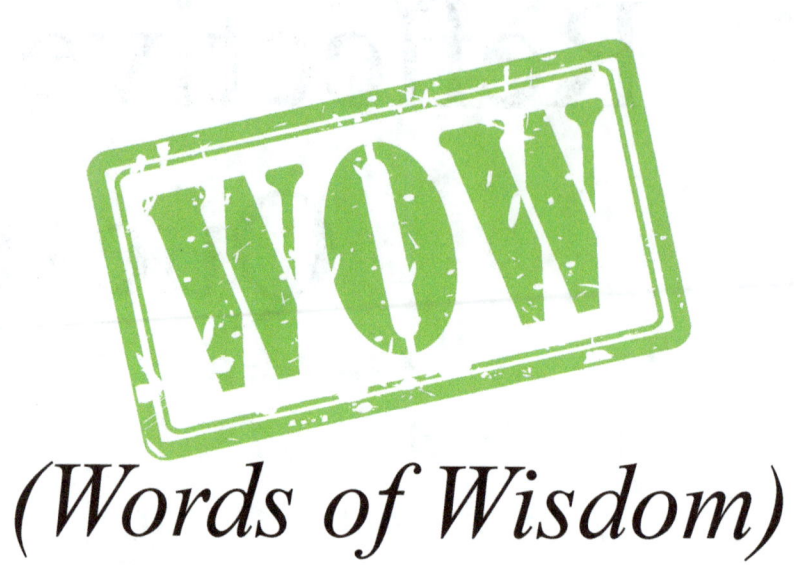

(Words of Wisdom)

What is more important to you; happiness AND peace or happiness OR peace?

With an equally yoked person, you will have both happiness and peace most times. There will be some rough periods; however, the commonalities can help you overcome them. To be unequally yoked means there is an imbalance that needs to be fixed. This imbalance can cause you to have happiness but not always peace, or days of peace with no happiness. These times will be felt by both parties, but one side may feel it more. Not to say there are not times when both will experience peace and happiness, but they don't last long nor do they occur often. However, you can work to be equally yoked; it will just take an equally conscience effort.

Give Me A.... **F**

Principle Forever

Defined: *Lasting or permanent.*

Forever is composed of nows.
— Emily Dickinson

In a world where everything is remembered and everything is kept forever, you need to live for the future and things you really care about.
— Eric Schmidt, University of Pennsylvania Commencement Address, 2009

Why...

Your actions today determine if your tomorrows are lasting & happy or short & miserable. Your relationship is similar to the work of a farmer who has planted seeds for harvesting. In order for the seeds to properly grow, the farmer has to tend the field after planting the seeds. Attentiveness helps to make sure the crops are bountiful. However, if they don't pull the weeds and kill the bugs the crop attracts, then the harvest will fail. The same is with any relationship. To make it last, you have to tend to it by rooting out issues & problems that may develop. You also have to actively water the relationship to establish firm rooting and successful growth. Without the proper cultivation of the relationship, as with the farmer's field, it can be filled with weeds of doubt, roots of distrust and die altogether. Plant seeds of good faith, well-doing and happiness, and tend to them daily in order to produce a healthy relationship.

Reflective Questions

What have you done lately to plant a seed of happiness for bad times? When you think of your mate, do you smile? When they think of you do they? Why?

A Few Lines...

F

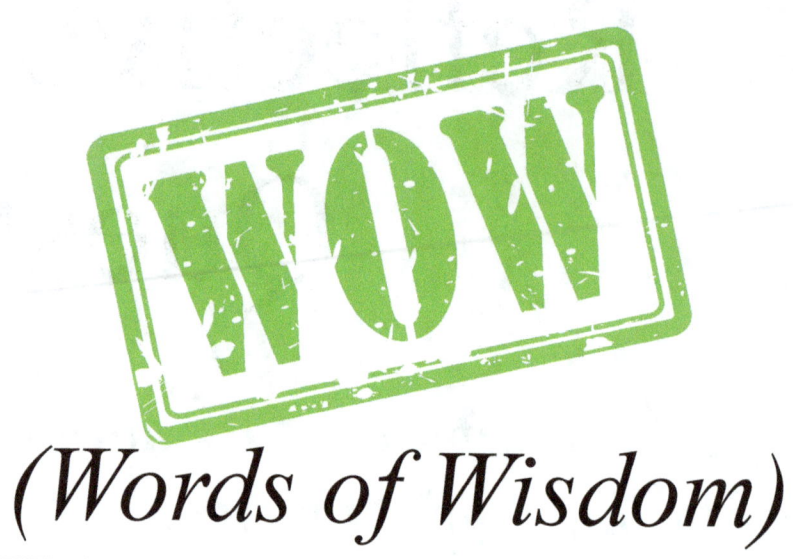

(Words of Wisdom)

If what you do today is what makes tomorrow worthwhile with others, why wouldn't the same apply to yourself? Yes, it is important to do things that make your mate happy, but self-happiness is just as urgent. The first law of nature is self-preservation. Make sure you do things to keep yourself smiling, or one day you will be looking at an empty shell of yourself. It is pointless to make someone else happy if you are not happy yourself. Find out what motivates you and do more of it.

If forever is composed of many NOWs,
you should constantly do things each day
to ensure tomorrow and next year are successful for you!

Give Me A.... **G**

Principle Genuine

Defined:  *Possessing the claimed or attributed character, quality, or origin; not counterfeit; authentic. Actually produced by or proceeding from the alleged source or author; sincerely and honestly felt or experienced*

Two Thoughts...

The genuine love of your life is the one that makes your heart beat a little faster, the person you are constantly trying to impress, the person whose voice you need to hear, and whose smile you love to see; the person you do the little things for. But most importantly, it is the person you feel complete with.
— Rashida Rowe

*Genuine people don't come around too often.
If you find somebody real enough to stay true. Keep them close.*
— Unknown

Why...

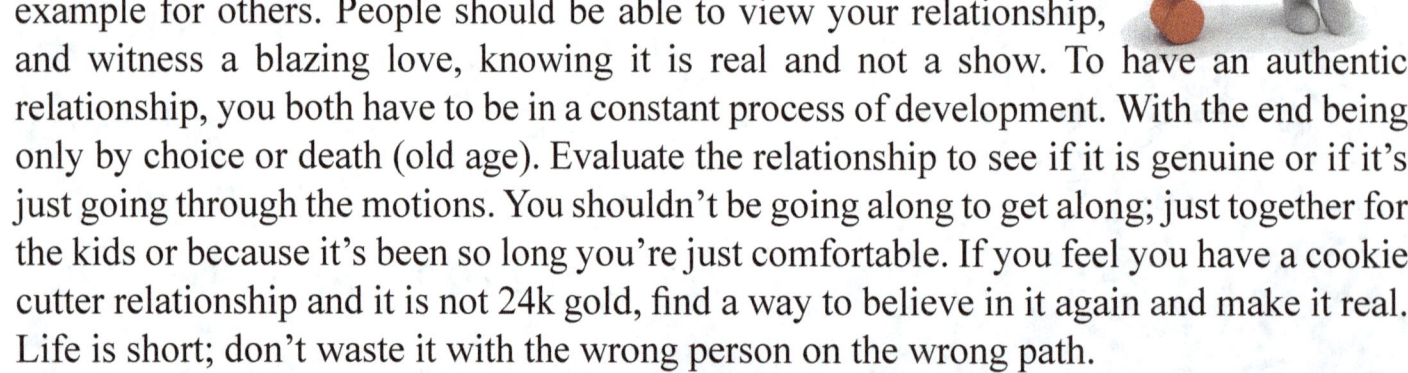

The authentication of any item is long and cumbersome. In hopes that the end results mark it genuine, and the value of it priceless. The same should be stated about your relationship; it is priceless or can be an example for others. People should be able to view your relationship, and witness a blazing love, knowing it is real and not a show. To have an authentic relationship, you both have to be in a constant process of development. With the end being only by choice or death (old age). Evaluate the relationship to see if it is genuine or if it's just going through the motions. You shouldn't be going along to get along; just together for the kids or because it's been so long you're just comfortable. If you feel you have a cookie cutter relationship and it is not 24k gold, find a way to believe in it again and make it real. Life is short; don't waste it with the wrong person on the wrong path.

Reflective Questions

Why do you believe your mate is the "one"?
Do they believe the same about themselves or you?
How long are you willing to continue working and/or waiting on that belief for it to become reality?

A Few Lines...

G

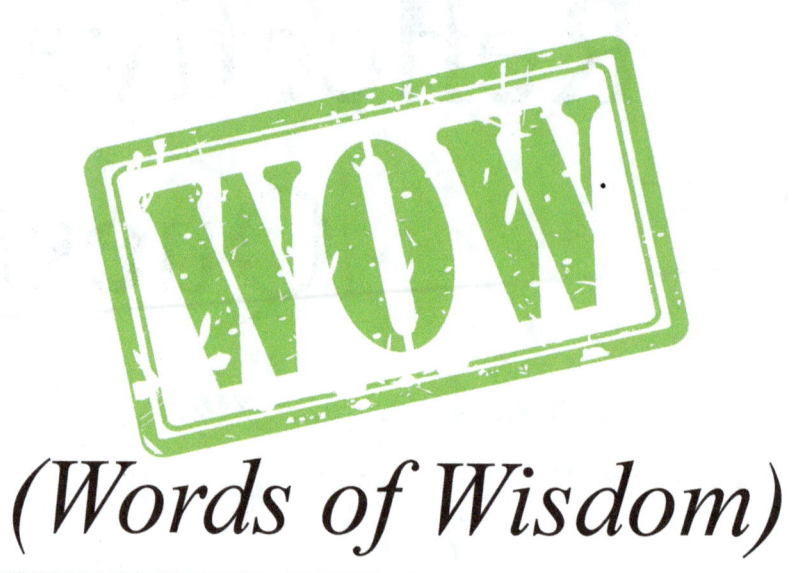

(Words of Wisdom)

Many people often find themselves in doubt, questioning their mate. At some point you should ask yourself, *"What is causing me to stay in a relationship if I don't think things will get better?"* Why are you choosing to be with someone whose values are not up to your standards? The process of authentication in court is done via direct questioning. However, to get the right answer you must ask the right question. The same is with your relationship; make sure you ask the right questions to get the right answer in order to make proper decisions.

Give Me A.... H

Principle

Heaven

Defined:  *The place where God lives and where good people go after they die according to some religions; a place that is very pleasant or good. A spiritual state of everlasting communion with God; a place of peace*

You couldn't relive your life, skipping the awful parts, without losing what made it worthwhile. You had to accept it as a whole – like the world, or the person you loved.
– Stewart O'nan

Do not await heaven above if we have failed to create it on earth.
– Unknown

Why...

Heaven is that feeling you get when you wake up next to your loved one for the first time and you realize your heart is safe... That feeling is the way your relationship should feel at all times. It is a feeling of safety and reassurance in your relationship, self, and in your mate. Yet, to obtain this feeling, you may have had to go through hell to get to heaven. But, once you're there, you don't want to go back. So, to prevent going back to the feeling of hell (or losing the one you love), do things to make it feel like heaven is right here on earth. Spend time with your mate. Do things they like, and find ways to create lasting great memories. Don't wait till you "get older" or "when you get things in order in your life." Quit putting off for tomorrow what you can do today, for tomorrow is not promised to anyone. Understand you WILL go through challenges, but even during those periods your mate should know you are where their home is. If you choose to focus on the negative, it will create more imbalances in your relationship. But, if you choose to stay positive, heaven will always be with you. *Heaven and hell are right here on earth and are just a reflection of the condition or state of mind you are currently living in.* Choose wisely!

Reflective Questions

What is heavenly (a good feeling) to you?
What is heavenly to your mate?
When is the last time you did this for each other?

A Few Lines...

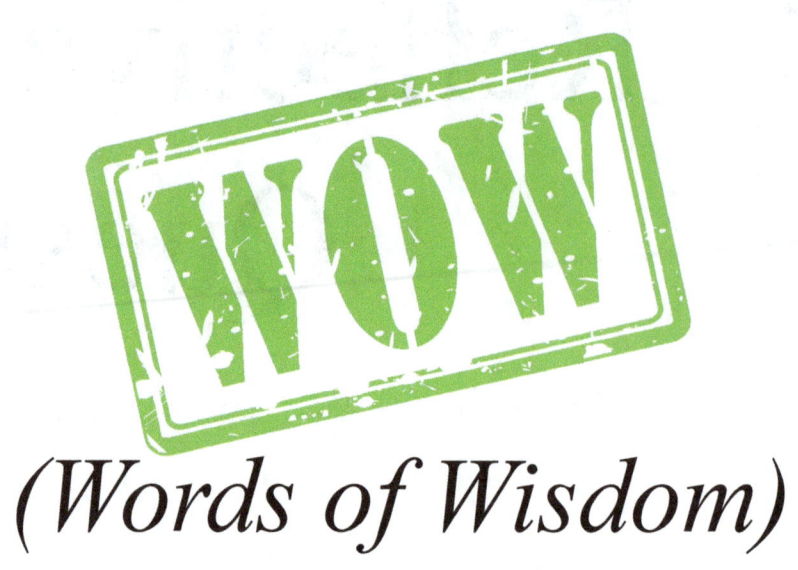

(Words of Wisdom)

I once read a quote that read, *"If one expects their mate to be an angel in their life, then they must first create a heaven for them."* Heaven for you might not be the same definition of heaven as your mate. Though you may enjoy romantic strolls in the park or cuddling while reading a book, that may not be a form of enjoyment for your mate. Find out what's their happy place and help to create it. You can choose whether or not to participate in it; just don't disturb it with your version of how it should be.

Give Me An... I

Principle Identity

Defined: *The fact of being whom or what a person or thing is designed to be.*

*Never forget what you are, for surely the world will not.
Make it your strength. Then it can never be your weakness.
Armour yourself in it, and it will never be used to hurt you.*
– George R. R. Martin, A Game of Thrones

*Unless we base our sense of identity upon the truth of who we are,
it is impossible to attain true happiness.*
– Unkown

Why...

Before you can fully accept yourself, you first have to know and remember who you are. Once discovered, do not change who you are to make someone else happy. It is said, *"Women get in relationships for the man's potential while men get in relationships for who the woman is."* As a result, many times the male in the relationship is happy and living stress-free while the woman is miserable and living unfulfilled. Don't come into a relationship trying to change a person to what you *"think they can be."* **Here are two reasons: 1) A person will only amount to the status they set for themselves. 2) Most times they wind up changing or stressing you out in the process.**

"I Am" is the most powerful two-word phrase you can speak. For whatever you attach to it, you are striving to become. Pay attention to your mate's descriptions of them self before and during the relationship. From this, you will have a sense of where the relationship is headed. Always aim to maintain a true identity and love of self. At the end of the day, it is always you staring back at you when you look in the mirror. If you don't like what you see, change it!

I

Reflective Questions

Who are you?
What makes you unique in comparison to others?
What makes you continue to desire this particular mate you are with?

A Few Lines...

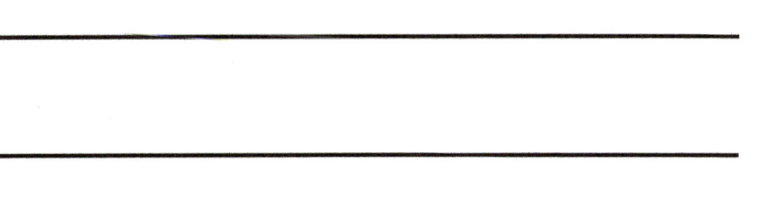

_____
_____
_____
_____
_____

I

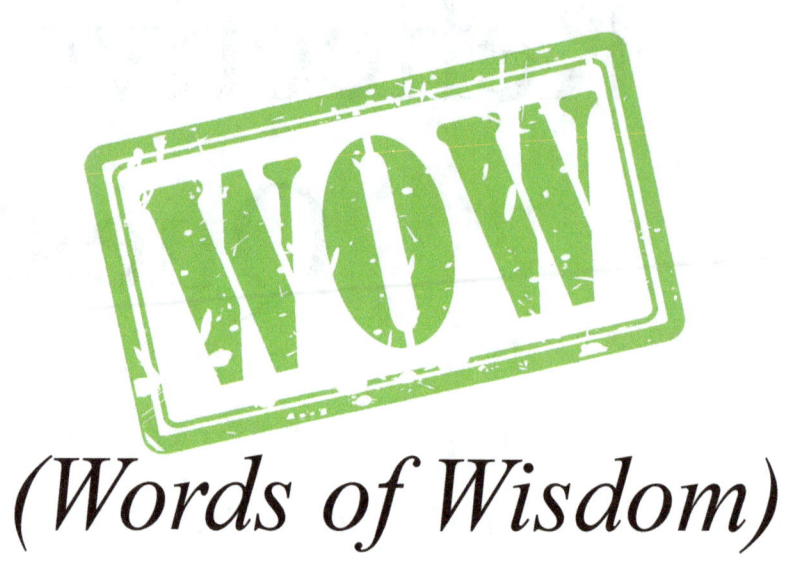

(Words of Wisdom)

A bee can't be a spider, and a spider can't be an ant. These three magnificent creatures' abilities are the most studied of God's creation. They know who they are, what their selective roles in nature are and how to master them. That's what makes them successful. Once you know who you are and accept your purpose, you will stop giving discounts to people for your time. Stop accepting people in your life who are below your character level. Know what you want when you begin your interactions with a person. If they don't fit the criteria, don't waste your time. Understand that time is more valuable than money. You can generate and lose money then generate more, but you can never regenerate time.

Give Me A.... **J**

Principle Journey

Defined: *A distance, course, or area traveled or suitable for traveling; an act of traveling from one place to another; something suggesting travel or passage from one place to another*

The journey of 1,000 miles begins with the first step...
— Unknown

The beautiful journey of today can only begin when we learn to let go of yesterday.
— Dr. Steve Maraboli

Why...

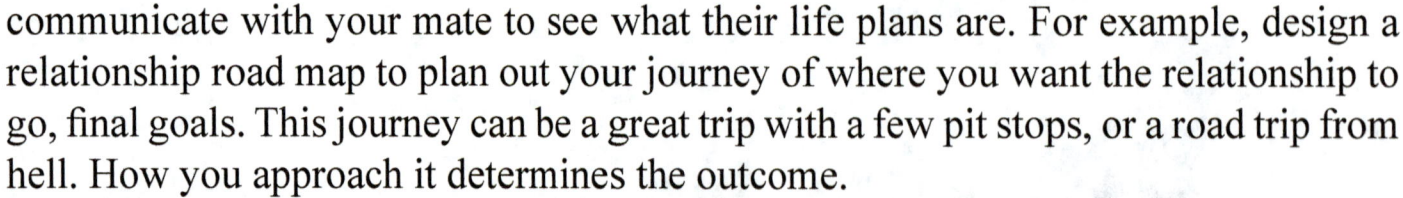

While a trip is often considered short and enjoyable; an enduring journey may have numerous obstacles and route changes. However, the journey often leads to a profound & life changing destination. The same should be true of a romantic relationship, it should not be short-term. If you believe that it is, why are you in it? You should communicate with your mate to see what their life plans are. For example, design a relationship road map to plan out your journey of where you want the relationship to go, final goals. This journey can be a great trip with a few pit stops, or a road trip from hell. How you approach it determines the outcome.

Final thought: *"A sailor without a destination cannot hope for a favorable wind."* You are the Captain of this vessel called Life, where are you headed?

Reflective Questions

How long do you foresee this journey lasting?
What are the intended final results of this relationship?
Does your mate share the same thoughts?

A Few Lines...

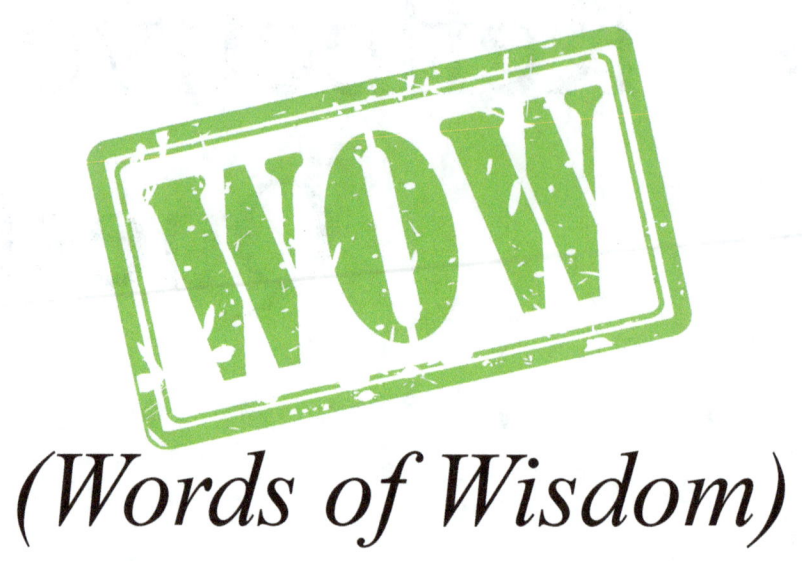

(Words of Wisdom)

"The fastest route between two points is a straight line... But the most memorable one may require you go off course."

The same is true of your relationship. You can live a long, safe and boring one (which is very unlikely), or a memorable fulfilling one. Understand that there will be peaks and valleys in the relationship. However, it is the steady and committed journey to your destination, wherever it may be, that makes it worth while.

Give Me A.... **K**

Principle

Know Your Mate

Defined: *A person who is perfectly suited for another in temperament. A person who strongly understands another in attitude or belief*

It's hard to stay mad at someone who knows how to make you smile.
— Unknown

You're not looking for perfection in your partner. Perfection is all about the ego. With soulmate love, you know that true love is what happens when disappointment sets in - and you're willing to deal maturely with these disappointments.
— Karen Salmansohn

Why...

It is said that many of the issues we encounter in any relationship stem from not TRULY KNOWING our mate. What makes the other person happy and sad? What motivates them? What are their life goals? Are they really a soul-mate rather than a life partner? The fulfillment of any relationship is when there is utter happiness and peace between the two individuals. When you know what makes a person respond positively or negatively, you know how to avoid problems in that relationship. One should work to get to know the other person, such as remembering special days, small gestures that make them smile, their favorite flowers and colors, etc. This principle can be key to the longevity of a successful relationship, for there will be trying times. But it is the recovery that makes it last.

Reflective Questions

What do you know about your mate's happiness?
Are they truly happy or living a lie?
How much does your mate know about you? Why?

A Few Lines...

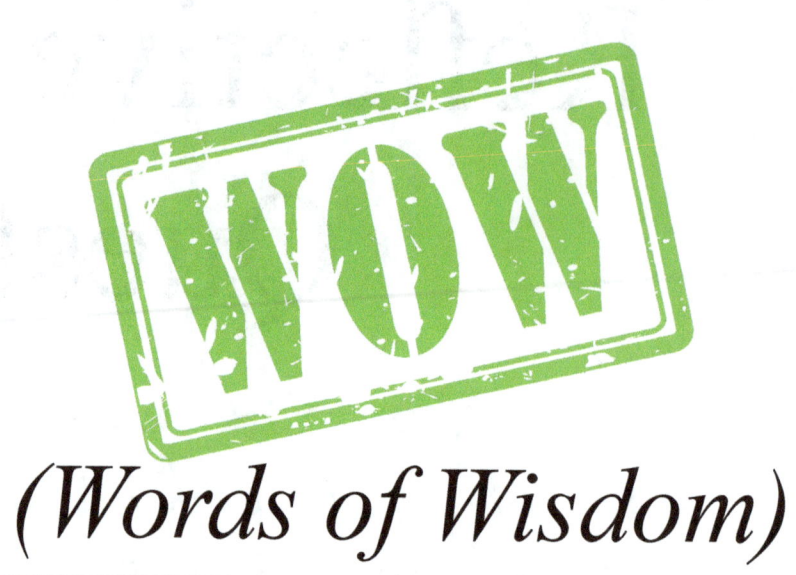

(Words of Wisdom)

Knowing your mate makes the relationship a little easier at times. When they are upset with you, knowing how to make them smile helps to ease tension in the relationship and can open the door for communication.

However, more importantly, you need to truly know yourself. The knowledge of self is what many of us lack, and that is where the problem begins. To know others is good, but to know self is better. If you can't make yourself happy or know how to encourage yourself, there will always be problems in your relationships that you will blame on your mate. However, once you get to know yourself, many of your outside problems will cease to be issues anymore.

Give Me A....

Principle L

Loyalty

Defined: *A strong feeling of support or allegiance.*

TWO THOUGHTS...

*Confidentiality is a virtue of the loyal,
as loyalty is the virtue of faithfulness.*
– Edwin Louis Cole

*Loyalty means I am down with you whether you are wrong
or right. But I will tell you when you are wrong and help you get right.*
– Unknown

Why...

Because this book is designed to help define and build a foundation for your love and your relationships, loyalty was chosen for a principle of understanding. Loyalty is essential to both partners; it is another degree of trust and a bonus to dedication. Loyalty means you are with this individual and most importantly you believe in them. This is not a feeling that comes overnight. Just as it takes time to develop trust, it also takes time to develop loyalty. However, the results of loyalty are sweeter than candy. Loyalty allows each to move freely without the worry of the commitment level from their mate. When this level is present, even in questionable circumstance, you will seek facts before allowing emotions to determine your outcome. *Many times the eyes and mind see what we feel at the moment rather than the reality of the situation.* In a truly loyal situation, it is only through their actions that the relationship can be damaged. True love cannot exist without loyalty.

L

Reflective Questions

Have you fully supported your mate in their goals? How?
Do you understand the difference between being loyal and being foolish?
What are the deal breakers in the relationship?

A Few Lines...

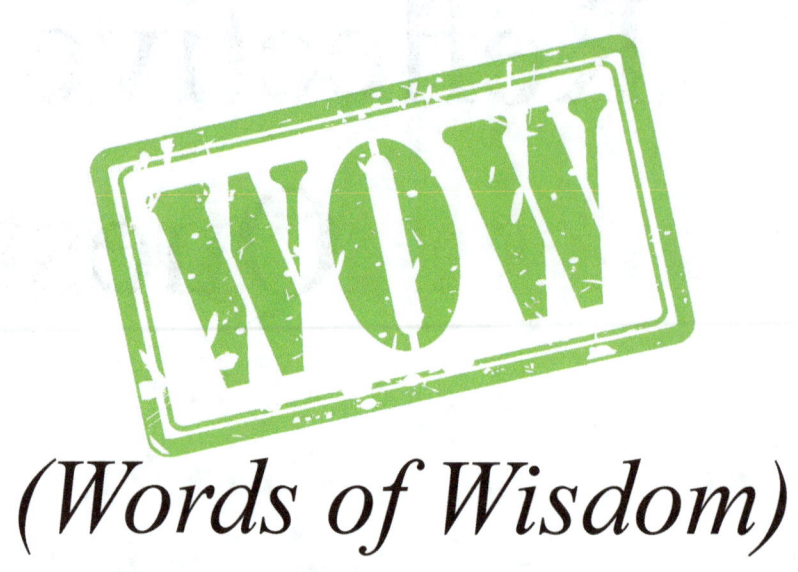

(Words of Wisdom)

There is a difference between Loyalty and Stupidity…

Know and understand the difference. It is beautiful when one can stay in the relationship through thick and thin. However, to be with someone who constantly disrespects or harms you is not true love. It is a misplacement of loyalty. Mutuality is key in a relationship, both parties should be receiving and returning loyalty. Happiness is what you should always seek; peace of mind should follow.

Give Me A.... M
Principle Motivation

Defined: *The act or process of giving someone a reason for doing something. The condition of being eager to act or work for something. A force or influence that causes someone to do something*

*You're the main character of your life's story.
Give your audience not only something to look forward to,
but something to be inspired by.*
— Kevin Ngo

*If you want to live a happy life,
tie it to goals not to people or an object.*
— Albert Einstein

Why...

My father once stated, *"Live for yourself and not for others, for if that person dies then what do you have to live for..."* Often people place their motivation and hopes in other people or things, instead of goals. Hence, when that relationship ends or that object crumbles... that motivation and hope fades. In a healthy and successful relationship, the growth of the relationship should be one of the biggest motivating factors. Communication is important in this principle, for goals should be discussed in the relationship, quite often. Have common as well as separate goals, and be supportive of them even on the days when you are at odds. Setting motivational goals can help you both find common ground, and build a stronger bond. What are we striving for?

Reflective Questions

What motivates you daily in your own personal life?
What about in the relationship?
What is the intended success story that motivates this relationship?

A Few Lines...

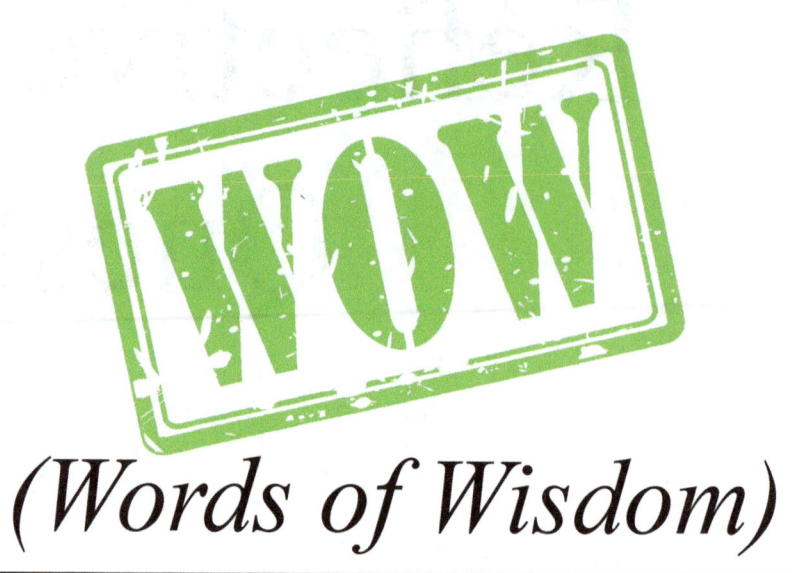

(Words of Wisdom)

There is no greater feeling than that of the happiness when you have accomplished a personal goal. Setting goals for yourself and the relationship can bring happiness to you both. Do things that encourage you all to work together (i.e. exercise, cooking dinner, paint & sip, yard work). Competition is good, but friendly competition is better because it helps in building a bond. You don't want to beat your partner at everything, over time it can make them feel defeated and resist interaction with you. The goal is always to have fun and to build a bond you can grow on.

 *Give Me A....* **N**

Principle

New Day

Defined: *The beginning of something*

Two Thoughts...

Today is a new day. Don't let your history interfere with your destiny! Let today be the day you stop being a victim of your circumstances and start taking action towards the life you want. You have the power and the time to shape your life. Break free from the poisonous victim mentality and embrace the truth of your greatness. You were not meant for a mundane or mediocre life!

— Steve Maraboli

Never use your failure yesterday as an excuse for not trying again today. We may not be able to undo damages, but we can always make a new start.

– Unknown

Why...

Every day that you live represents a new opportunity to express yourself in ways you haven't before. Treat every day with the newness of the first day. Strive to love your mate every day with the same enthusiasm you had in the beginning. Life is not guaranteed to anyone, for what is present today can be a memory tomorrow.
Hence with your loved one, you should not constantly hold on to issues that may arise, either find a way to get past them or let the relationship go. Holding on to issues with the other person, having misplaced trust, and hate does nothing to advance either of you. It only causes problems for you mentally and physically over time. Let it go! Learn how to always keep the relationship fresh and look for new ways to keep it together, instead of destroying it.

Reflective Questions

What are some of your biggest issues in the relationship?
Why do you choose to not let it go?
How is holding on to them helping you all grow?

A Few Lines...

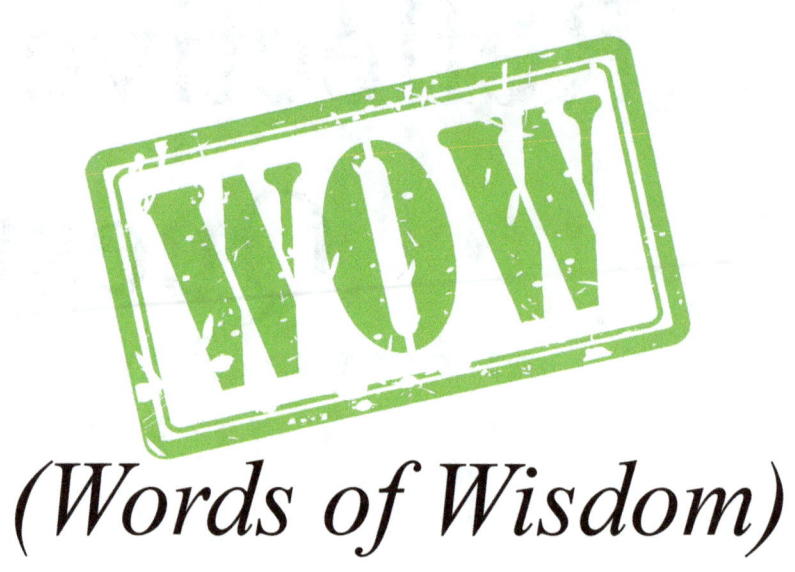

(Words of Wisdom)

The key to a long and successful relationship is a short memory...

(Re-read that sentence and take a moment to let that soak in.)

There are no reasons to continuously fight or argue with loved ones. The troubles of yesterday need to be left there. If they carry over to today, it should be only because the issues are still present. Then today should be about resolutions to solve those issues so they can be eradicated. As I was once told, *"If it's not life or death, there is no need to fight. However if it is life or death, you still need to talk to come to a logical answer."*

So there is still never a reason to fight your mate.

Give Me An... O Principle

Open Mind

Defined: *Being willing to consider new ideas; unprejudiced.*

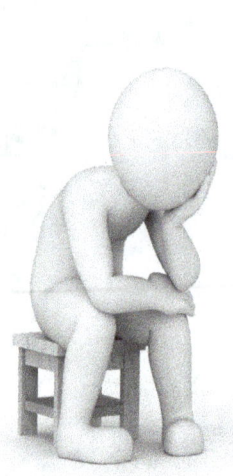

Those who cannot change their minds cannot change anything.
– George Bernard Shaw

We are trained in this society to reject anything that we do not understand. Elevate your mind.
– Unknown

Why...

You should have a **DEGREE** of open-mindedness with thoughts and opinions that come from your mate. Be willing to be open when your mate comes to discuss their concerns and ideas with you. You don't have to accept every idea that they bring, but you should be open to listening to them. Allowing your mate to express their concerns or ideas keeps the relationship open and alleviates secrets.

A bonus of being open-minded is that your mate gets a chance to know you better. They also discover the limits that the significant other is willing to go beyond their comfort zone. Proper communication is still the best key to the relationship's longevity. If that key component to the relationship breaks down you allow room for someone else to enter, along with their thoughts and ideas.

Reflective Questions

How open are you to new ideas in the relationship?
What are your limits?
What are your partners?

A Few Lines...

_____

_____

_____

_____

_____

o

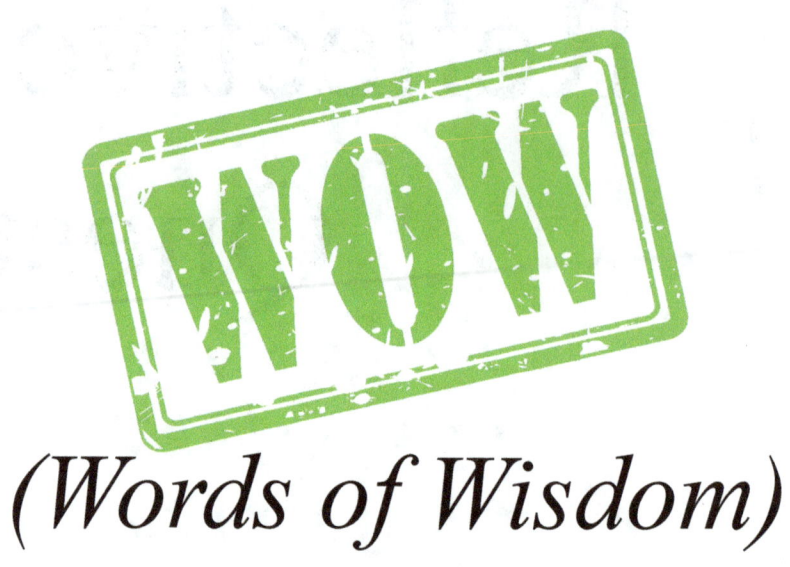

(Words of Wisdom)

Being open in a relationship is like reading a good book, you will always find a reason to return to it. While being open invites communication between you and your mate, being excessively open can cause problems. Moderation is the balance to everything, know when to share your opinion and when to stop and take a moment to self. Not everything needs to be shared and not everything needs to be known by everyone.

You're a mature individual, use your discretion.

The Letter P has Two Principles
that require understanding for growth.
1) Past
2) Patience

Part - 1

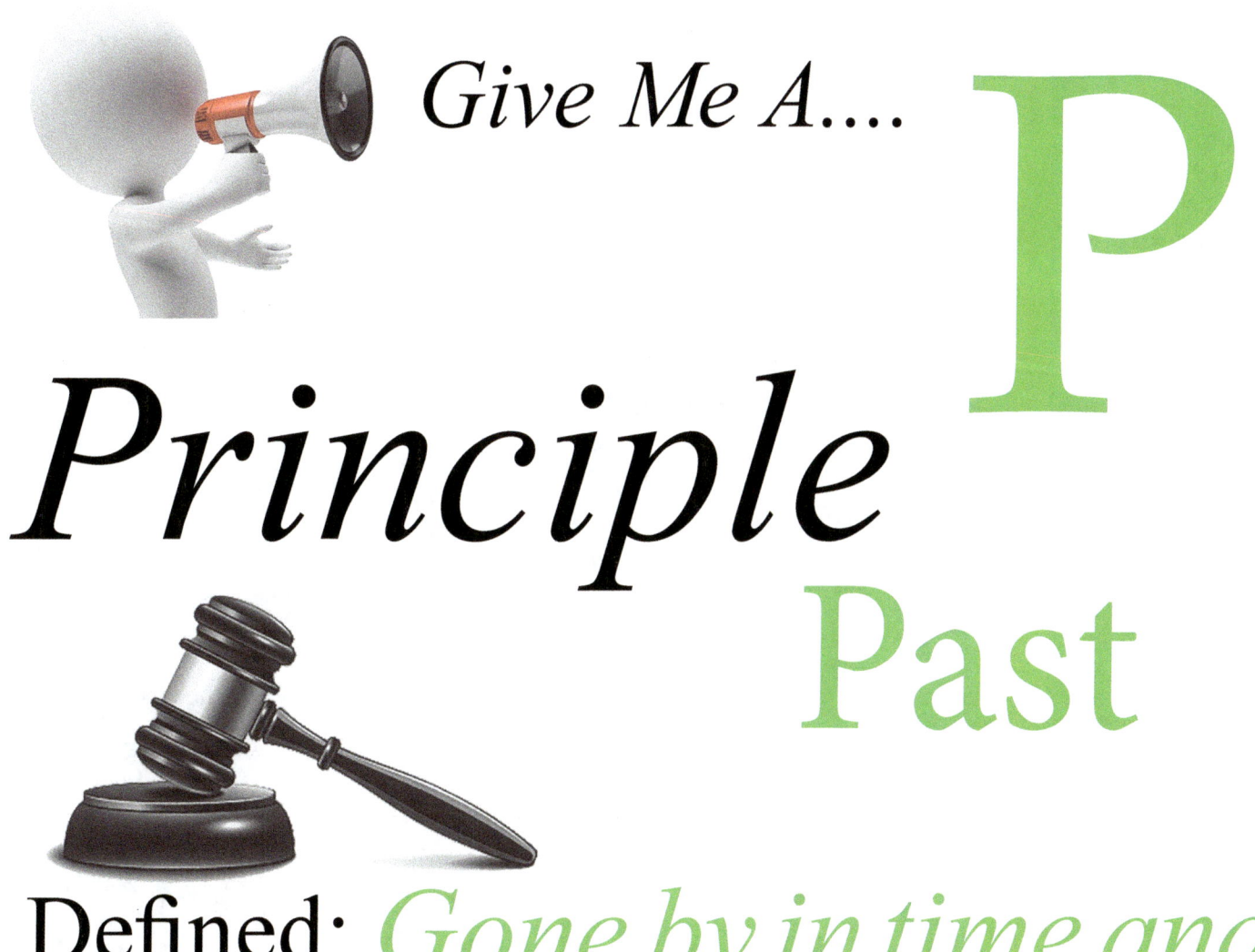

Give Me A.... **P**

Principle

Past

Defined: *Gone by in time and no longer existing*

*Life can only be understood backwards;
but it must be lived forwards.*
– Søren Kierkegaard

*The past is the past, leave it there!
The past is finished. There is nothing to be gained by going over it.
Whatever it gave us in the experiences, it brought us was something we had to know.*
– Rebecca Beard

Why...

A person's history does not always determine their future nor does their present represent their past, life is about development and growth. Just as in order to see tomorrow, you have to live through the mistakes of today. In order for you to produce pure gold, you have to burn off the impurities that surround it, the same is with human nature. The gospel singer Donnie McClurkin said it best "*A Saint is just a sinner who fell down and got back up.*" Growing with a person over time their past will come out, not all of it being the best. However, you shouldn't get upset and leave them because most times you didn't know that person at that stage of their life. Also, it may have been a necessary phase of development in their life. Understand for that person to be the person you desire today, those choices were necessary learning steps for them. Remember the past is just that, it cannot be changed or altered, only the future can. So if you allow their past to change your future with them, you didn't deserve them anyway. (Circumstances may vary)

Reflective Questions

*If you are still being hurt by your past,
can you leave the pain in your past?
Are you willing let it go? What's stopping you?
When will you start to let go and heal?*

A Few Lines...

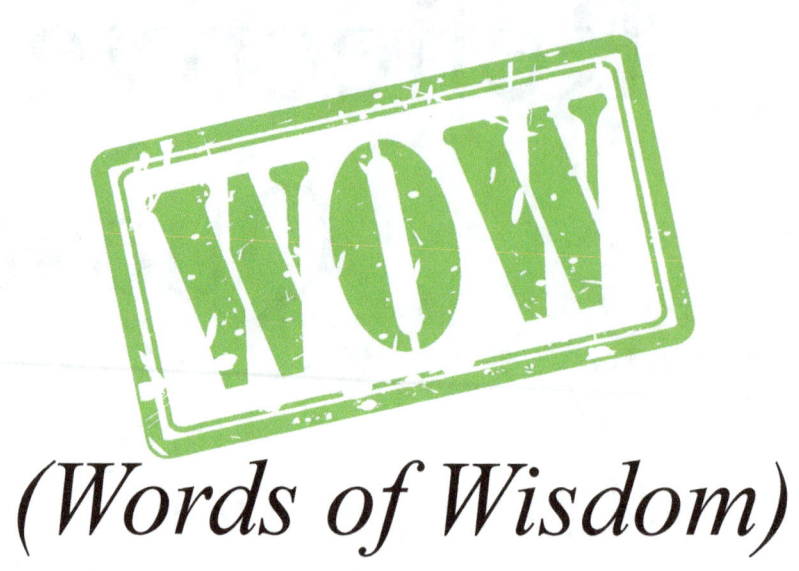

(Words of Wisdom)

Apply the words from the Ghostbusters theme song to your life, "*I Ain't Afraid Of No Ghost.*" Ghosts from the past can't harm you unless you allow them to by your actions. If it happened in the past, leave it there. If it happened while in the relationship and you chose to leave it in the past, again leave it there. This is the equivalent of burying a dead animal and later digging it up to bring it back to life. The subject has passed, let it stay there. It can bring you no good by walking around with a dead subject around your neck. It soon begins to stink and cause your mate and others to avoid you. Think of life as riding in a car, the rear-view mirror represents the past while the windshield represents the future. Don't confuse the two; focusing on the small images in your past can cause you to wreck the beautiful image ahead of you.

Part - 2

Give Me A.... **P**

Principle Patience

Defined: *Bearing pains or trials calmly or without complaint; steadfast despite opposition, difficulty, or adversity*

*Patience is not the ability to wait,
but how you act while you're waiting...*
– Unknown

Anything worth having... is worth waiting for...
– Unknown

Why...

No one is made to be like you, nor will they be exactly as you want them to be. That's called being a clone or a slave, neither equates to a healthy relationship. Patience is needed as you both make mistakes DAILY, most of which should be forgiven and tossed into the *Sea Of Forget*. When you accept a person in your life, you must accept their strengths and their flaws. Have patience as you grow together to become a better couple and not to abort the process. Dr. King said it best, "*Be patient with people and impatient with progress.*"

Reflective Questions

What bothers you the most about your mate?
Why do these things bother you?
Are these your personal issues or ones that they can change?

A Few Lines...

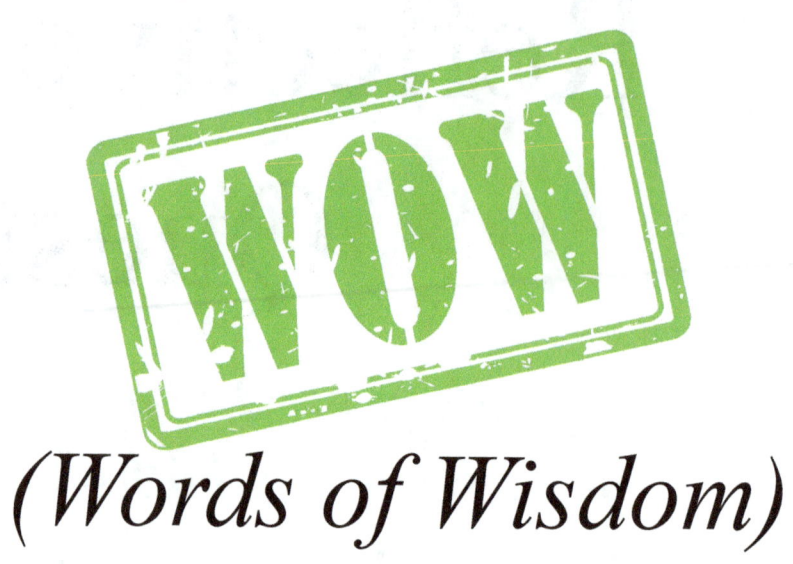

(Words of Wisdom)

Almost every Prophet in the spiritual books was told by God to wait. Why? Because He had something better in store for them and good things come to those who wait. My mother would often say, *"Focus on the Goal and Not the Gold in Life."* The goal of obtaining the gold in your relationship will only be reached after mining it with patience.

Millions of paper dollars are made in one day, but it takes three million years to make a real diamond. Just as it takes an average of three minutes to make a fast food meal, but three days to make most Thanksgiving dinners. Both will fill you up, but which one is more nourishing for you? The value in all of these examples and your relationship appreciates with time.

Give Me A....

Principle

Q

Quit Complaining

Defined: *Make changes or be quiet*

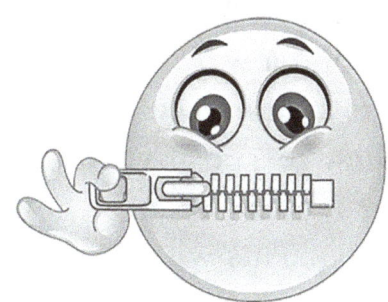

*If the grass looks greener on the other side.
Stop staring. Stop comparing. Stop complaining and
start watering the grass you're standing on.*
— Unknown

*Smile and stop complaining about the thing you can't change.
Time keeps ticking whether you're happy or sad.*
— Unknown

Why...

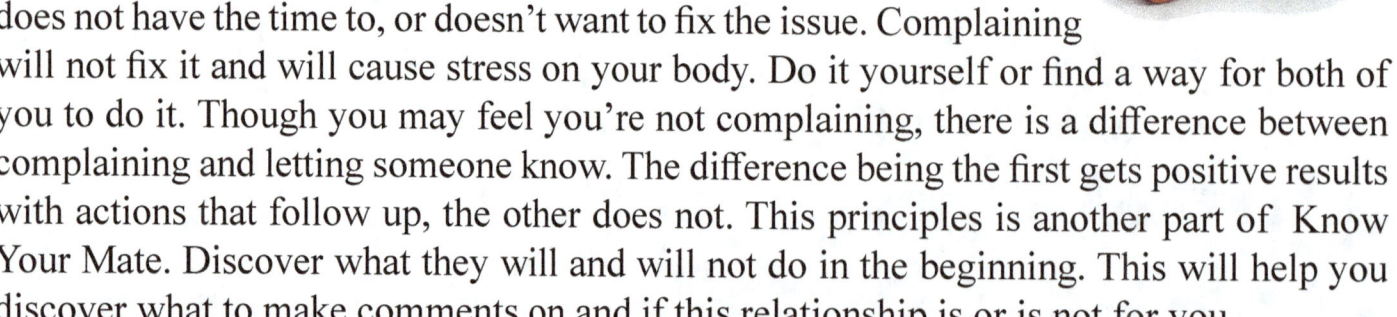

Nagging is one of the unhealthiest habits in any relationship. After a while, it causes the other person to block the mate out or leave. If something is out of place or has not been handled in the manner that you want, fix it yourself! Either the opposite party doesn't know how to, does not have the time to, or doesn't want to fix the issue. Complaining will not fix it and will cause stress on your body. Do it yourself or find a way for both of you to do it. Though you may feel you're not complaining, there is a difference between complaining and letting someone know. The difference being the first gets positive results with actions that follow up, the other does not. This principles is another part of Know Your Mate. Discover what they will and will not do in the beginning. This will help you discover what to make comments on and if this relationship is or is not for you.

Reflective Questions

How often are you nagging your mate?
How long does it last and why? Does it work?
Is there any other way to motivate them
to do what you want?

A Few Lines...

(Words of Wisdom)

If A + B does not = C, complaining about A will not change the formula or its outcome. Either find a way to resolve A or change the formula. Saying the same thing over and over expecting new results has a higher success average with teachers at school than individuals in a relationship. Decide if this issue is that important. Learn to choose your battles. If you want to see change, motivate the individual to change, nagging does not help.

Give Me A....

Principle R

Rest

 *Be placed or supported so as to stay in a specified position. An instance or period of relaxing or ceasing to engage in strenuous or stressful activity.*

Men seek rest in a struggle against difficulties; and when they have conquered these, rest becomes insufferable.
– Blaise Pascal, Pensées

*Almost everything will work again
if you unplug it for a few minutes, including you.*
– Anne Lamott

Why...

This principle of Rest is so highly important that on the 7th day, God did it! When the two of you are striving to be one, issues may arise daily in the relationship and outside of it. A suggestion is that each day before you deal with each other, take a moment to relax and separate yourself from the world. For example, sit in the car before going in the house after work to recapture your thoughts of you and your mate. Leave the outside world there. Then, whatever issues are at home, strive to work them out before going to bed. If you just keep sweeping unresolved matters "under the rug," you will look up one day to see a pile of hidden issues that one of you is harboring.

Not just communication, but Proper Communication is key! To keep a healthy and open relationship, find a way to communicate in a healthy manner when one or both of you is upset. Strive not to go to bed with issues between the two of you, try to talk it out so that you never let distance grow between you. Also, learn how to take needed time from each other; not too long though.

Reflective Questions

How often do you all discuss the day or your thoughts?
How often do you take a few minutes to yourself?
What are you doing with this time?

A Few Lines...

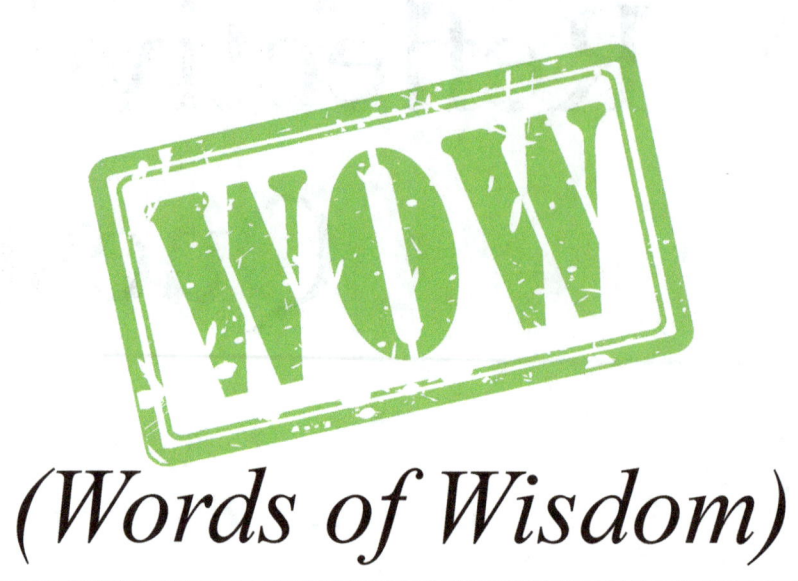

(Words of Wisdom)

A picture is worth a thousand words; yet, with proper rest, one can probably express a million. Learn to take time to yourself daily without your mate. This helps to keep sanity and peace in the relationship. With proper rest in the relationship, the picture of it to others & self always stays bright and attractive. Be a light that others see when they look at you and your mate. That comes from you being each other's mental place of rest in good and bad times.

Give Me A.... **S**

Principle Strength

Defined: *The quality or state of being strong. A good or beneficial quality or attribute of a person or thing.*

We are only as strong as we are united, as weak as we are divided.
– J.K. Rowling, Harry Potter and the Goblet of Fire

Don't be afraid of your fears.
They're not there to scare you.
They're there to let you know that something is worth it.
— C. JoyBell C.

Why...

Learn and understand where your strength lies and how to use it, not for the advantage of self, but for the advancement of the relationship. Do not become stagnant because of comfort. Have the strength to know when to stand for something in the relationship, and when it's best to step back and choose another route. Strength, just as communication, comes in many forms. One of the major strengths we have to master is bridling of the tongue, for it is as a two-edge sword.

When there is strength in a healthy relationship, both parties work together for a commonality. However where there is weakness, you see the constant feuding and competition to outdo one another. Knowing your strengths and how to use your strengths for good is what makes a successful relationship. There are many forms of strength in the relationship; for example knowing when to listen or to disagree, when to press an issue or not, when you should stay or to leave. Know that somethings are for a season versus for a lifetime. Nothing lasts forever; it comes to an end at some point.

Reflective Questions

Have you ever analyzed your relationship?
What are the Strengths & Weakness?
How often do you choose
the "high road" and avoid a battle?

A Few Lines...

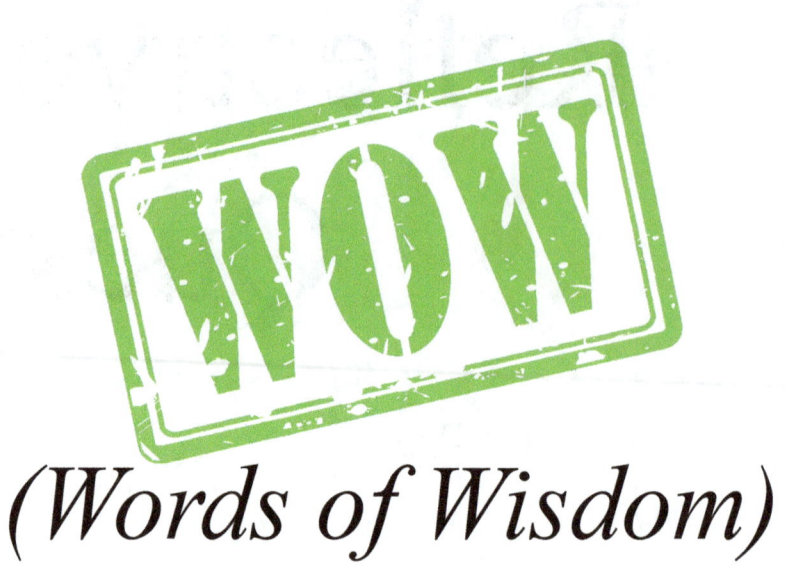

(Words of Wisdom)

Sometimes, the biggest strength is shown when one chooses to back down though they may be right. A person who learns how to skillfully maneuver in a relationship will pick and choose their battles, and ultimately prevail with the most strength in the relationship. You can always beat down your mate or lash out at them, but how does that grow their trust in you or desire to become more open and affectionate?

"Sometimes by losing a battle you find a new way to win the war."

Give Me A.... T

Principle Trust

Defined: *Firm belief in the reliability, truth, ability, or strength of someone or something. Confidence placed in a person by making that person the nominal owner of property to be held or used for the benefit of one or more others.*

*I'm not upset that you lied to me;
I'm upset that from now on I can't believe you.*
– Friedrich Nietzsche

To be trusted is a greater compliment than being loved.
– George MacDonald

Why...

If you are in a relationship where there is NO TRUST..., there is no reason to be in the relationship.

You can't be in a full-time relationship with part-time trust. Either you have to find a good reason to be in the relationship or discover the reason you want to leave. To sleep with someone and not trust them is the equivalent to sleeping with the enemy. Make a choice. If you are going to be in the relationship, BE IN IT! If there is question or hesitation for an extended period of time on too many subjects... LET IT GO!

T

Reflective Questions

*How often are you doubting (questioning) your mate's response? Why?
Do you treat them how you want to be treated or talked to?
Do you know how they want to be treated?*

A Few Lines...

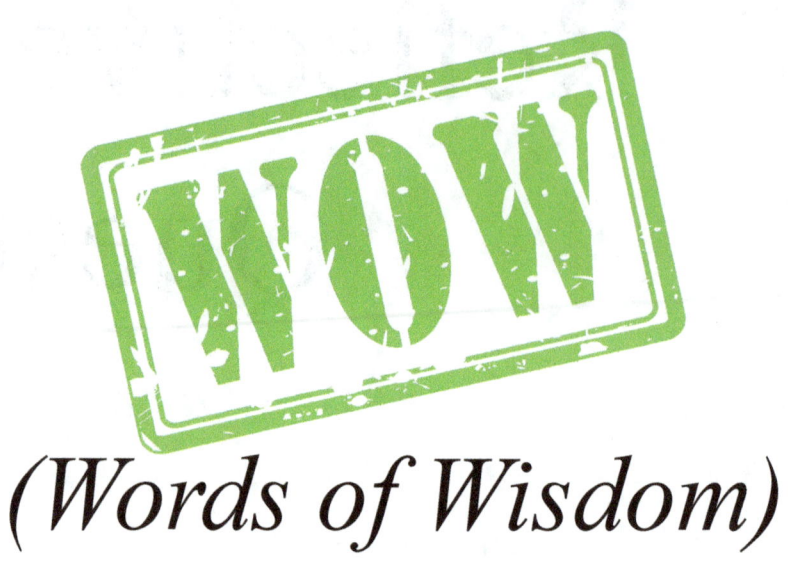

(Words of Wisdom)

Trust starts and ends the same way... with YOU.

Showing and presenting your trust, at all times, helps to build a bond only you can break. Having no trust in each other is the equivalent of building a house on quicksand. It's bound to sink at some point. When the trust has been broken, either find a way to mend it so it's truly put in the past or you should decide the next best move for you. "Putting it in the back of your mind" or holding on to issues against your mate, will still lead to a breaking point for you or them. Harboring issues is the like holding on to a hot stone with the intention of throwing it... yet you never do. You're only hurting yourself... let it go!

Give Me An... U

Principle Unique

Defined: *Being the only one of its kind; unlike anything else.*

Being different isn't a bad thing.
It means you're brave enough to be yourself.

— Unknown

"Do you think I'm wonderful? She asked him one day as they leaned against the trunk of a petrified maple. "No," he said. "Why? Because so many girls are wonderful. I imagine hundreds of men have called their loves wonderful today, and it's only noon. You couldn't be something that hundreds of others are."

— Jonathan Safran Foer, Everything Is Illuminated

Why...

Is all snow made up of the same material... *Yes*.
However, every snowflake is made unique and is not shaped like any other. So is your relationship.
Is it between two people?
Can you claim to be a match made from heaven?
Can you claim it to be an example of how all relationships should be? All of these you might possibly say yes to. However, your relationship is not like any other, not your parents, friends, siblings or some celebrity couple. Listen to the advice that is given, but know how to discern what works best for you. I was once told, *"ALL people like to be happy... But not all people WANT TO SEE YOU HAPPY..."* Think on that for a moment.

Reflective Questions

Who has the ideal relationship to you, why?
Do you compare your life and relationship to theirs?
*Are you carving out your own relationship path
or following someone else's?*

A Few Lines...

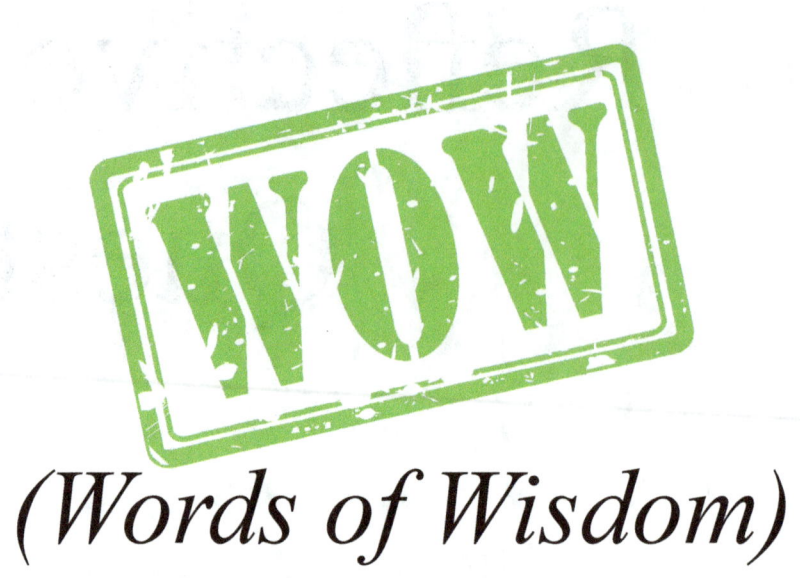

(Words of Wisdom)

If all roses were red and all flowers were blue, what would make them special...

If you and your mate are constantly comparing yourself to the Joneses, what makes you unique? What brings about happiness in a relationship is when the individuals in it do what makes them happy with each other. Those small dorky things that make you two laugh with each other, expand on them and do not worry what others think. Be an original in a world full of carbon copies.

 *Give Me A....* **V**

Principle

Value

Defined: *The regard that something is held to be deserved. The importance, worth, or usefulness of something.*

*When you learn how much you're worth.
You'll stop giving discounts.*
– Unknown

Knowing what you value and how much you value it, is the fire that illuminates the dark. The world is full of so many lights that others want you to walk towards. Meditating helps keep your eyes firmly fixed on the light of what you value.
– Bill Adams, The Fire Lessons of Life

Why...

A long life is not promised to anyone, learn to value other's time. When someone goes out of their way to make others happy, it is done by choice not by force. Appreciate when your mate does things for you. Even when they do small things, like making dinner or taking out the trash, a simple "Thank you, dear" or an appreciative hug goes a long way.

These small things can make Valentine's Day feel as if it's every day. A person wants to feel as if they are valued and not just a part of the decor of your life. A valued person can be considered an asset in your life, while the random person is a liability subtracting from your growth. The same for you, you have to choose your position in your mate's life, and what role you will play. You can have a relationship of a Coach and a Quarterback or that of a Wide receiver and a spectator. One works together towards a common goal while the other is a separate unit.

Reflective Questions

Do you feel you are valued in the relationship?
What have you done to be valued or to bring value?
Are you acting as an asset or
a liability to the relationship? How?

A Few Lines...

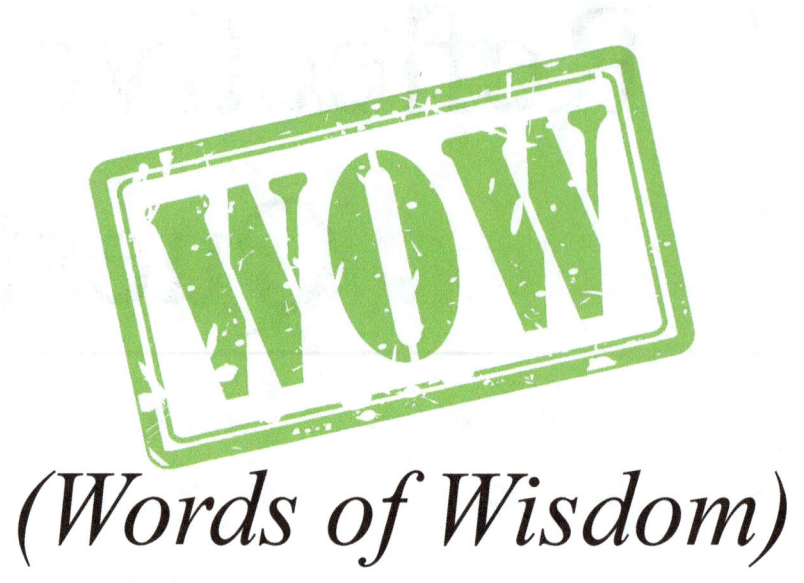

(Words of Wisdom)

A good name is worth more than gold, just as a positive thought inspired by your mate can be worth the same. Be that one thing that your mate can always depend on for peace and happiness, guide them to be that one for you. The value of happiness and peace in a lasting relationship is priceless.

 *Give Me A....* **W**

Principle

We

Defined: *Used by a speaker to refer to himself or herself and one or more other people together.*

We accept the love we think we deserve.
– Stephen Chbosky

What we see depends mainly on what we look for.
– Sir John Lubbock

Why...

When you two agree to be with each other, there is no more "You" and there is no more "I", it is now "WE." You both should be working for the future benefit of each other, not just self. When you think of yourself, you should think of the other person too. Just as when they think of themselves they should think of you and the effects of every decision. Always remember that when you enter a new committed relationship, married or not, this is a new bond. You are no longer an island or peninsula. You are forming a country with each one of you representing a state. The more people in the family, the more states and the bigger the country. In order for your country to survive, they have to act as a whole and understand the roles of each person.

Reflective Questions

When making decision do you think of how it will affect your mate?
Who is represented by "WE" in this relationship?
Does your mate agree?

A Few Lines...

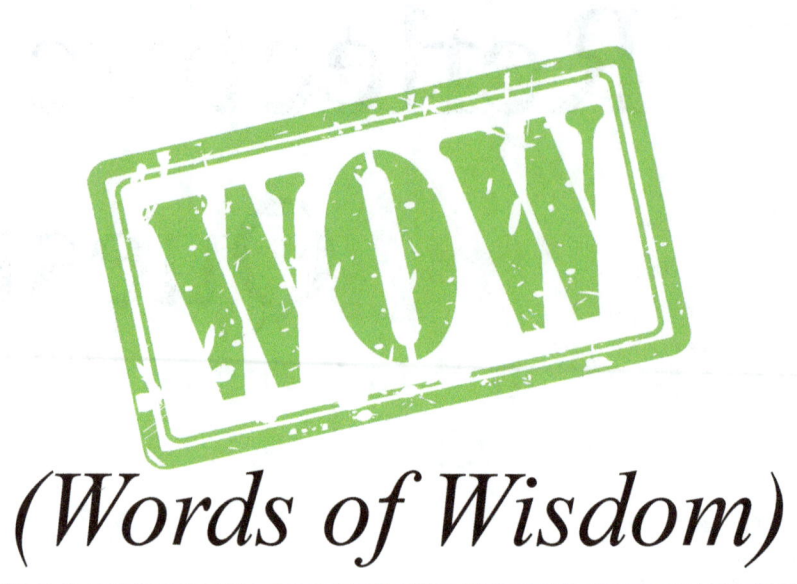

(Words of Wisdom)

"We" is one of the strongest two letter words you will ever use. Be careful of who you attach yourself to and why you're doing it. This attachment can hinder you or advance you. The value of teamwork is best explained in the African Proverb, *"If you want to go fast, go alone. If you want to go far, go together."* So if you are now a "We", the question becomes, *"In what direction or destination are you both traveling and what are the plans when you both get there?"*

Give Me A....

Principle X

X-Ray

Defined: *The ability to see through a thing clearly*

True love can blind you but at the same time if you let it, it can also open your eyes.
– Nikhil Saluja

Transparency is removing the mask and revealing who you really are. It is getting beyond the surface to what is really going on in your heart.
– Unknown

Why...

When you begin to fully commit to any relationship, one of the main things you **NEED** to have is clarity of heart and mind. *If you carry the same bricks from your past relationship to your new one, you will end up building the same house that fell apart before.* If you bring the same doubt, mistrust, and other issues from the past into the present relationship, this one won't last either. With that thought in mind, it is always good to take time to yourself before entering into a new relationship. If the person is for you, they should be willing to wait with understanding, so you will have a promising future.

Once in the new relationship, be clear in your intent with each other and with your thoughts. Do not try to hide from your own thoughts. Be open with yourself and willing to discuss things that may be hindering you in order to get past them. Be the truthful person you seek in the relationship and the favor should be returned.

Reflective Questions

What issues in the relationship did you least expect to continue to arise and why?
How are you working to get past it?
Have you tried a new approach?

A Few Lines...

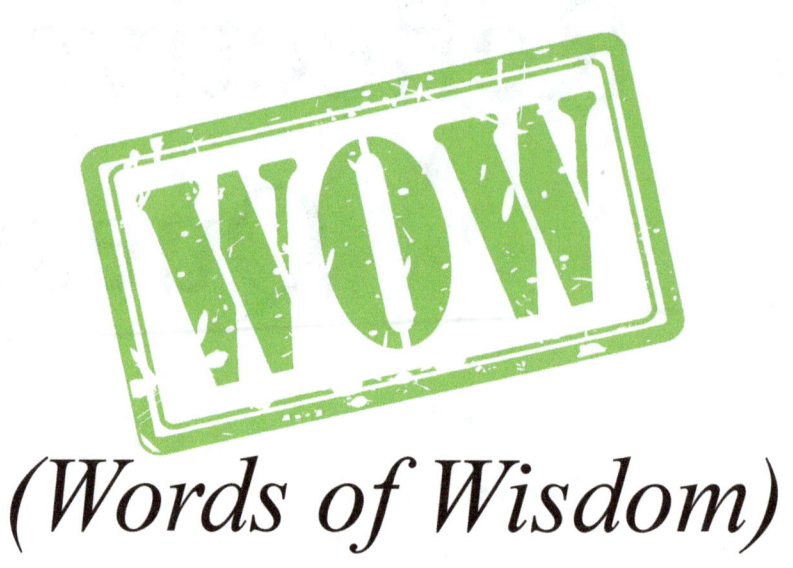

(Words of Wisdom)

Your mate can not read your mind. That mock conversation you just had with yourself in your mind; that was supposed to be with your mate. You never really had it with them, so they still do not know what the issue is when you see them again. Open your mouth and learn to PROPERLY COMMUNICATE! That does not include using vulgar language, innuendos about one another, or physical harm. Learn to express yourself and your feelings in a way that relays your point clearly so your mate can understand. If not, you will have that same mock conversation in your head again next week.

Give Me A....

Principle Y

Youthful

Defined: *Young in the relationship; youth is the time of life when one is young. "The appearance", freshness, vigor, spirit, etc.*

Youth is happy because it has the capacity to see beauty. Anyone who keeps the ability to see beauty never grows old.
— Franz Kafka

I've never talked to our guys about being young. That's an easy crutch to fall on. You really just have to come in and build the spirit up of your team by working them every day, showing them examples of what they've done and reinforce their work.
— Scott Brooks

Why...

As new blood brings a steady flow of life and growth into a body, youthful energy does the same to a relationship. A relationship gets old; not by age, but by the lack of new energy and spirit that is brought to the relationship. Many times, you have seen older couples with more life between them than younger couples. It's because they have found reasons to live and happily express themselves together. Get out of the thoughts of what others may think of you and concern yourself with what your mate may want to do. Every year for your anniversary, plan to do something adventurous as a couple that you have never done before. Make lasting memories while putting a new life into the energy that is already present.

Y

Reflective Questions

Have you done anything to bring new life into your relationship? When is the last time you've done something you haven't done before? What is an activity you all love to do together that makes you both happy? When is the last time you did that?

A Few Lines...

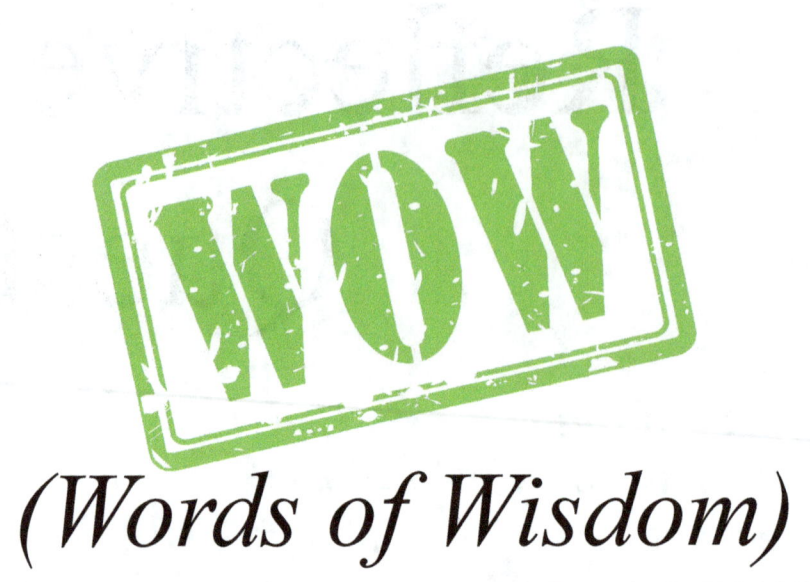

(Words of Wisdom)

Youth is an attribute, a way of thinking, a reaction to life, it is not a matter of age or looks...

Once a month, plan something that you all can do to keep the spirit young and alive between you. That is what keeps the love fresh. Quit making excuses for not living, *they are only tools of incompetence used to build monuments of nothing that lead nowhere.*

Give Me A.... Z

Principle Zealous

Defined: *Ardently active, devoted, or diligent; full of, characterized by, or due to zeal. Eagerness and ardent interest in pursuit of something*

One person with a divine purpose, passion and power is better than 99 people who are merely interested. Passion is stronger than interest.
– Israelmore Ayivor

Worship is action. Worship is not lazy, boring and sad. Worship is zealous, famous and joyful.
– Mac Canaza

Why...

Be zealous, a degree past passionate, in all that you do towards and with your mate. Even if it is something you do not enjoy but they do (i.e. walks in park, reading books, certain TV shows). Find some enjoyment in their passions because it is the thing your mate loves. Your actions toward them should also be full of zeal, so they never have to question, *"Does this person love me?"* The thought should always be, *"To what extent doesn't this person love me?"* However, always remember the difference between loyalty and stupidity in your actions.

Reflective Questions

How does your mate know you love them?
How do you express your passion for them outside of the bedroom? (Fighting does not count)
What is the degree of passion you have to see that your relationship will last?

A Few Lines...

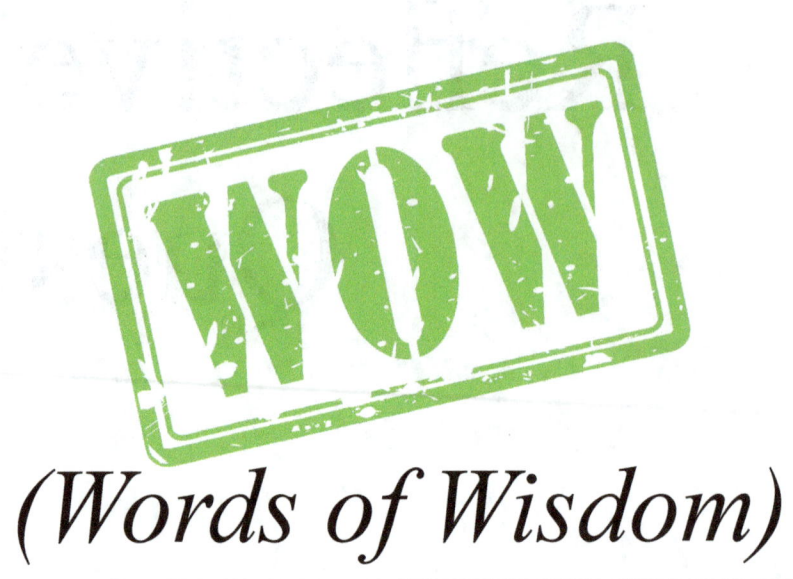

(Words of Wisdom)

There is a difference in zealous and jealous and that involves trust. In zeal, you trust your mate and are happy they are developing and you want to help them succeed. While jealously is rooted in mistrust. In short, one is positive and the other is not. Keep a healthy outlook toward your mate and your relationship, but never put them above yourself. Show excitement in the things you do together. Have genuine joy about the things your mate is trying to achieve.
Be zealous about your time together.

Bonus Principle

Principle

Rise Up

Defined: *To elevate One's Self and thinking.*

When you rise up in faith knowing that God is with you and for you, all doubt and fear has to leave your life.
– Unknown

It is when we fall that we are given the opportunity to rise up and reach new heights.
– Unknown

Why...

A good friend once corrected me about "being in love". I told her, "I look forward to falling in love one day…" To which she corrected me and said, *"We should not fall in, we should Rise Up in it."* To rise is to elevate yourself and the relationship you are in.
If something fell, it is because most times you were careless with what you were holding. When you pick that object up, you become more aware of it and try harder not to lose it again. The same should apply to your relationship. Do not fall into it and be lazy. Pick it up and cherish every moment you have in it. Push daily to elevate it higher than it was the day before. This ensures happiness, longevity and a reason to want to be in the relationship. Hence from now on, do not "Fall in Love", you should "Rise Up In It!"

Reflective Questions

The first time you "fell in love", what were the mistakes made? Have you made them again?

To rise means to grow and develop, have you all discussed what you want to grow into?

When mistakes are made in the relationship, do you all use them to grow from them or do you cast judgement and hold it?

A Few Lines...

*

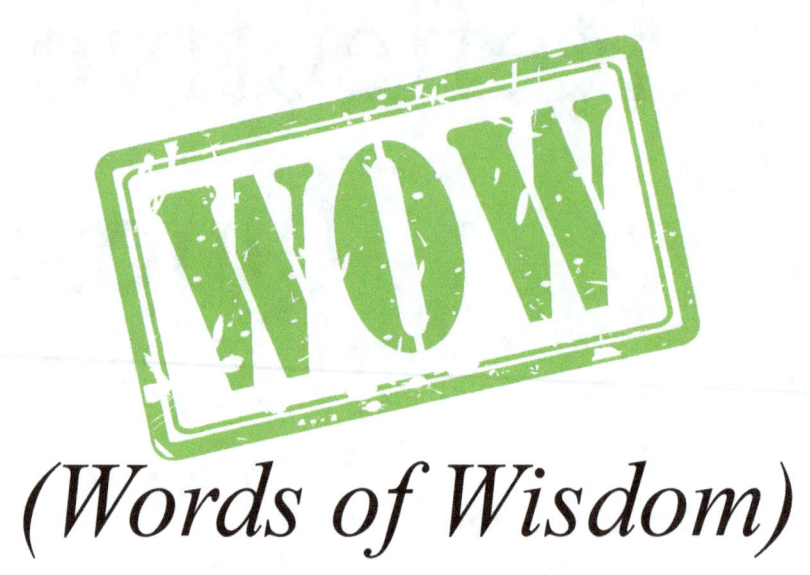

(Words of Wisdom)

An Angel is not one who fell from Heaven. That would mean they did bad and was sent backward. An Angel is one who rose from the dirt, doing well enough to ascend above others.

Let your love change daily; a constant struggle to be better today than you were the day before.

Closing Thoughts

I can be your Tinkerbelle and you can be my Peter Pan and we can run away together off to Never Never Land...
– Unknown
(Make your own world enjoyable with your mate.)

*What is the one thing in a relationship that
always moves and never stops?
Goes forward but never backward?
Can feel like it stops, but if so you have just lost it?*

Time....
Always make some for the other person.
- Yusuf A. Muhammad

Additional Space For Notes

Additional Space For Notes

_____

_____

_____

_____

_____

_____

_____

Cite References

[1]Forward - Unknown; [2]Letter A - The Honorable Elijah Muhammad; [3]Letter B - African Proverb; [4]Letter H 1st - A. Temeca Magee; [5]Letter H 2nd - The Honorable Minister Louis Farrakhan; [6]Letter H 3rd - Unknown; [7]Letter I - Unknown; [8]Letter J 1st - Lean Tee, M.D.; [9]Letter J 2nd - Yusuf A. Muhammad; [10]Letter M - Steven Muhammad; [11]Letter N - Yusuf A. Muhammad; [12]Letter N - Abdul Allah Muhammad; [13]Letter P2 - Margaret A. Muhammad; [14]Letter S - Donald Trump; [15]Letter U 1st - Yusuf A. Muhammad; [16]Letter U 2nd - The Honorable Minister Louis Farrakhan; [17]Letter X - Unknown; [18]Letter Y - Unknown; [19]Rise Up - Rachel Chanyah Faulkenstein

All quotes have been properly cited.
If not cited, it is an original from Yusuf A. Muhammad.
Please Quote Properly
Definitions are from Merriam Webster

www.ingramcontent.com/pod-product-compliance
Lightning Source LLC
Chambersburg PA
CBHW081155290426
44108CB00018B/2564